Table of Contents

Welcome to Scotland's Puddings, Desserts and Sweet Treats.

Thank you so much for picking up this book and wanting to discover the joys of Scotland's Puddings, Desserts and Sweet Treats. As a proud Scot I am delighted to share with you some of my favourite sweet dishes that I have enjoyed making over the years and that have given joy to friends and family alike.

Scotland has a long tradition of baking and steaming puddings and recipes, like these have been handed down from generation to generation (maybe not the deep fried Mars Bar, that's a recent invention). Many of these recipes are hundreds of years old and reflect the simple ingredients that would have been available before the invention of supermarkets, like honey, oats and fresh raspberries. I hope you enjoy these recipes and you enjoy eating them as much as I have over the years.

~ **Margaret Mochrie**

Check out my first book **"The Wee Scottish Recipe Book"**

Festive Tipsy Laird

Tipsy Laird is on old favourite for my family especially on Christmas Day. The dessert, which is similar the English Sherry Trifle, was, and still is, affectionately known in my house as Christmas Day's second dessert. Like most families celebrating on Christmas Day we would have Christmas pudding, but after a wee 'barley' (rest from the gluttony) we would have a some Tipsy Laird as the second pudding of the meal. Heavenly!

Ingredients:

1 Victoria sponge cake, sliced
300g raspberry jam
1 wine glass of sherry (cream or sweet amontillado)
2 tablespoons Drambuie, Glayva or other Whisky Liqueur
Home-made egg custard (my classic custard recipe is below)
300g raspberries
2 bananas (optional)
250ml double cream
1 tablespoon castor sugar
Toasted almonds

For the custard:

250ml milk
150ml double cream
2 egg yolks
50g castor sugar
1 or 2 drops of vanilla essence

Method:

Place the sponge in the base of a large glass bowl and spread with the raspberry jam. Mix the sherry and the Whisky Liqueur (Drambuie etc) and sprinkle evenly over the sponge allowing it to soak in. Next add a layer of raspberries and sliced bananas.

To make the custard, whisk together the egg yolks, sugar and vanilla essence until pale and creamy. Heat the milk and cream together in a saucepan until boiling point then stir into the egg mixture. Once it is well blended, return to the pan and stir continuously over a low heat until the custard thickens.

Pour into a dish and allow to cool. When cool, pour the custard over the layer of fruit, spreading evenly. You can of course buy some tinned or cartoned custard but its always best to make your own.

Next whip the double cream, add sugar to sweeten and spoon on top of custard.

Decorate your Tipsy Laird with toasted almonds. Refrigerate for 1-2 hours then serve.

Traditional Clootie Dumpling

The Clootie Dumpling is a Scottish boiled pudding that has been around for hundreds of years. The word Clootie refers to the cloth the dumpling is cooked in. This is delicious served hot but can be sliced when cold and spread with jam for an afternoon treat.

Ingredients:

125g (4oz) suet, finely chopped
250g (8oz) self raising flour
1 tsp baking powder
125g (4oz) Scottish Oatmeal
75g (3oz) brown sugar
250g (8oz) currants/ sultanas mixed
1 tsp each of cinnamon and ginger
1 tbsp golden or maple syrup
3 eggs
1 tbsp buttermilk or milk

To Prepare the Cloth:
Half fill a large pan with water and bring to boil. Wet a large piece of white cotton or linen cloth in very hot water and squeeze out excess water. Dust with flour (which will help form the skin).

Method:

Mix the syrup in a little buttermilk until fully dissolved. Add this sweet liquid to all the other ingredients and mix to a soft dropping consistency.

Place this mixture into the centre of the prepared cloth, draw up the edges and tie with string leaving a little room as the Clootie Dumpling will expand as it cooks.

Drop into the boiling water and cook for 3-4 hours, topping up the water level as it cooks.
Serve warm with homemade custard or brandy sauce.

Selkirk Black Bun

Black Bun is a little bit like the better known Christmas cake but without the icing and marzipan. Instead the 'cake' is baked with a pastry crust which is rather delicious. This is traditionally served on Hogmanay (New Year's Eve) with a wee dram of single malt whisky.

Ingredients:

For the Filling:

200g plain flour, plus a little extra for dusting
200g raisins
400g currants
1 tsp ground mixed spice
1 tsp ground ginger
100g dark muscovado sugar
100g chopped mixed peel
½ tsp bicarbonate of soda
1 tbsp Scotch Whisky
1 egg, lightly beaten
3 tbsp milk
A generous pinch of freshly ground black pepper

For the pastry:

200g plain flour
½ tsp baking powder
50g butter, chilled and cubed
50g vegetable shortening or lard, chilled and cubed

Method:

To Make the Pastry:

Place the flour, baking powder and a pinch of salt in a large bowl. Add the butter and shortening and rub in between your fingers until it resembles breadcrumbs. Stir in 4 tablespoons of cold water and mix to a soft dough. Cover with cling film and chill while you make the filling.

Preheat the oven to 180C/ 350F/gas mark 4.

Mix all the filling ingredients together in a large bowl, with enough milk to just moisten it.

Dust a clean work surface with some flour. Roll out three-quarters of the dough to a rectangle large enough to line the base and sides of a 900g loaf tin. Place into the tin and press up against sides, smoothing out any creases.

Pack in the filling tightly into the dough lined tin and press down well.

Roll out the remaining pastry to a rectangle large enough to cover the top.

Dampen the edge of the dough in the tin with water and press the pastry lid on top to seal then trim off the edges.

Bake in the oven for 2 hours. Allow to cool for 1 hour.

Remove the black bun from the tin, then cut into slices to serve.

Gorgeous Drambuie Ice Cream

If you have never tried Drambuie I urge you to go out and get some. The liqueur is a secret blend of malt whisky, honey, herbs and spices which is thought to have been invented by Bonnie Prince Charlie and the secret of how to make it given to the Clan McKinnon for helping him escape from the Isle of Skye.

Ingredients:

100g/4oz Caster Sugar
90ml/3fl.oz. Water
6 Egg Yolks
210ml/7fl.oz. Double Cream, lightly whipped
3 tbsp Drambuie

Method:

Add the water and sugar to a small saucepan, bring to the boil then remove from the heat and set aside.

Place the egg yolks in a heatproof bowl over a saucepan of boiling water and whisk gently until pale and creamy. Make sure the eggs do not get too hot and scramble.

Add the sugar mixture and continue to whisk until slightly thickened. Remove the mixture from the heat and continue to whisk until cool.

Add the Drambuie and the cream, mix well then transfer to an ice cream maker and freeze and churn for 20 minutes or according to the manufacturers instructions. Transfer to a freezer proof container and freeze until firm.
Serve with delicious baked or steamed puddings or simply enjoy on its own.

Mary's Dundee Cake

The origins of the Dundee cake are lost in the midst of time. It is believed that it may have been created for Mary Queen of Scots who insisted her cake was decorated with almonds instead of the more usual glacé cherries as she did not like cherries. The link to the great city of Dundee comes from a Dundonian marmalade producer who started to mass produce the cake in the 19th century.

Ingredients:

To makes 16 slices:

100 g (4 oz) currants
100 g (4 oz) seedless raisins
100 g (4 oz) sultanas
100 g (4 oz) chopped candied orange peel
25 g (1 oz) blanched unsalted chopped almonds
275 g (10 oz) plain flour
225 g (8 oz) butter
225 g (8 oz) light soft brown sugar
finely grated rind of 1 orange
finely grated rind of 1 lemon
4 eggs
whole blanched unsalted almonds to decorate

Method:

Grease and line a deep 20.5 cm (8 inch) round cake tin with greaseproof paper.

Mix all the dried fruit, peel and chopped almonds with the flour.

Cream the butter, sugar and orange and lemon rinds together until pale and fluffy. Slowly beat in eggs.

Fold in the fruit and flour mixture, then spoon into the prepared cake tin. Arrange whole almonds in circles on the top to decorate.

Bake at 170C / 325F / gas mark 3 for 2 1/2 - 3 hours or until firm to touch. If the top gets too brown, cover with paper. Leave to cool for 30 minutes before turning on to a wire rack to cool completely.

Delicious as a mid-morning snack with a cup of milky coffee.

Heather Honey and Whisky Mousse

Honey and whisky, my two favourite Scottish ingredients, come together in this delightful dessert to be made solely for the grown-ups.

Ingredients:

4 large eggs
4 heaped tbsp. heather honey
140ml whisky
400ml double cream
4 sheets of leaf gelatin, soaked in cold water

Method:

Place the eggs, honey and <u>100ml</u> of the whisky in a heatproof bowl over a saucepan of barely simmering water and whisk until the mixture is pale and mousse like. Set aside to cool.

Whisk the cream until stiff then whisk in the rest of the whisky.

When combined fold the cream into the egg and honey mixture.

Squeeze any excess water out of the gelatin and dissolve in a splash of hot water before stirring it through your mousse.

Divide the mixture between dessert glasses and put them in the fridge to set for at least 3 hours.

Garnish with a few fresh raspberries and serve with a piece of shortbread.

Black Treacle Pudding

This is another old recipe which goes back to the late 19th century. Back in those days, sugar was a luxury that only the very rich could afford so the more humble folk rarely got the chance to cook with refined sugar or golden syrup. Only the much cheaper black treacle, which was effectively a by-product of the sugar industry, was affordable so great puddings like this were created.

Ingredients:

110g butter
110g caster sugar
2 eggs lightly beaten
3 tbsp black treacle
The grated rind and juice of half a lemon
110g self raising flour

Method:

Cream the butter and sugar until light and fluffy. Gradually beat in the eggs.

Warm the black treacle with the lemon rind and juice.

Gently stir this mixture into the creamed butter and sugar then carefully fold in the sifted flour.

Spoon the mix into a large pudding basin.

Cover tightly with greased greaseproof paper and foil then steam for 1 1/2 hours

Check the pan frequently to ensure that it doesn't boil dry.

Serve the pudding hot with golden syrup and cream.

Margaret's Marmalade Cake

From the late 18th century right up to this day orange marmalade has a been one of Scotland's great culinary products. Legend has it that the industry started when a ship full of oranges from Spain was washed up on the shore not far from Dundee and rather than let all the good fruit spoil, marmalade was made on an epic scale and the Scots fell in love with the stuff. Scots being ingenious bakers soon incorporated marmalade into their cakes.

Ingredients:

115g/4oz softened butter
90g/3oz light brown sugar
2 eggs
225g/8oz self raising flour
½ teaspoon baking powder
Pinch of salt
Grated zest of an orange
3 tablespoons orange marmalade
3 tablespoons milk

Cake Topping:

1 tablespoon orange marmalade
Juice of 1 orange
Grated zest of 1 orange
Icing sugar

Method:

Cream the butter and sugar together.

Fold in the eggs.

Sift the flour, salt and baking powder and add slowly. Loosen the mix with the milk.

Add the zest and marmalade.

Spoon the mix in to a greased loaf tin.

Bake in the oven for 55-60 min on 180C / 350F gas mark 4

Leave to cool in the tine for half an hour then tip out on to a wire rack.

Once the marmalade cake has cooled on a wire rack, spread the top with marmalade. Make a drizzle from the orange juice, zest and icing sugar and cover the top of the cake in it.

Serve!

Simple Honey and Whisky Cake

Honey and whisky in a cake. What more is their to love about this piece of heaven.

Ingredients:

6 oz self raising flour
6 oz butter
6 oz soft brown sugar
3 beaten eggs
4 tablespoons whisky
Grated rind of a small Orange

For the Butter Icing:

6 oz icing sugar
2 oz butter
2 tablespoons clear honey
Juice from the Orange

Decoration: Toasted Flaked Almonds

Method:

Set oven to190C / 375F/Gas 5.

Grease two 7 inch sandwich tins.

Cream the butter and sugar together in a bowl.

Add the orange rind then beat in the eggs one at a time and whisk until the mixture is pale and fluffy.

Sift in half the flour and add the whisky.Fold into the mixture. Now sift in the remaining flour and fold in.

Divide the mixture equally between the two tins.

Bake for 20-25 minutes until light golden.

Turn out on to a wire rack to cool.

To make the icing, put the butter into a mixing bowl. Add the honey and one tablespoon of the
orange juice.

Sift in the icing sugar slowly and work the mixture gradually until the ingredients are combined.

Sandwich the cakes together with half of the buttercream.

Smooth the remainder over the top of the cake and decorate with the toasted almonds.

Traditional Macaroon Bars

Today all the fancy sweet shops, patiserries and bakers seem to be selling the multi coloured 'macaroons' which are completely different thing to the macaroon bars I had as a child. In Scotland a macaroon is a fondant type bar made from mashed potato (yes... mashed potato) and covered in chocolate and coconut.

Ingredients:

1 large potato
400-500g icing sugar
2-3 drops vanilla extract
300g dark chocolate
100g dessicated coconut

Method:

Boil the potato until soft. Drain, measure out 100g, then mash until there are no lumps, and leave to cool.

Put the cold mashed potato, vanilla extract and 100g of icing sugar in a bowl. Mix well until it turns to very thick, sticky paste. Keep adding the icing sugar, 100g at a time, mixing well after each addition, until you have a stiff white fondant.

Line a tray with greaseproof paper, put the fondant in the tray, and press flat. Cover with cling film and leave in the freezer for an hour.

In the meantime, toast the coconut in the oven by spreading thinly on a large baking sheet and cook in the oven at 150C / 300F gas mark 2 for around 5 minutes until the coconut is just golden. Keep an eye on it as it can burn easily. Remove from the oven and allow to cool.

Remove the fondant from the freezer. Cut into bars about 3 inches by 1 inch.

Melt the chocolate in a bowl above a pan of barely simmering water. Once the chocolate is melted and smooth, dip each bar into the chocolate, then roll in the coconut.

Transfer to a sheet of greasproof paper and allow to set.

Aunt Betty's Ginger Flapjacks

Where would we be in Scotland without the humble oat? When Samual Johnson wrote 'A Dictionary of the English Language' in 1746 oats were described thus "A grain, which in England is generally given to horses, but in Scotland supports the people." Without it there would be not porridge, haggis or Flapjacks (amongst many other things). These ginger flapjacks are my favourite Sunday treat.

Ingredients:

6 oz butter
8 oz porridge oats
4oz demerara sugar
1 level teaspoon ground ginger
1oz golden syrup

Method:

Set the oven to 170F / 325F / gas mark 3.

Place the butter, sugar and syrup together in a pan and heat gently until the sugar has melted.

Remove the pan from the heat and stir in the oats and ginger. Mix well leaving no dry oats.

Press this mixture into a greased 8 inch sponge tin and bake for 15 to 20 minutes.

Allow to cool then cut into slices, bars or wedges.

Delicious when served still slightly warm and chewy but are equally good when cooled.

Snowballs

I have fond memories of having these as a child. After church on a Sunday if me and my brother and sister had been very good we would get this as a treat after our family dinner. They were always so much fun to eat but very sticky and messy with the jam and the icing covering our faces. They used to be sold in all the local shops but today I rarely see them. Just as well I have this great recipe.

Ingredients:

For the cakes:

75g of caster sugar (6 1/2 TBS)
75g of self raising flour (11 TBS), sifted
2 medium free range eggs
Seedless raspberry jam

For the glacé icing:

200g of sifted icing sugar (1 1/2 cups)
2 TBS warm water
few drops vanilla
75g of sweetened dessicated coconut (about 1 cup)

Method:

Preheat the oven to 200C / 400F / gas mark 6.

Grease a large baking tray and dust with flour, shaking off any excess.

Break the eggs into a bowl and whisk lightly. Add the sugar and whisk until the mixture becomes thick, creamy and almost white in colour, about 8 - 10 minutes. Lightly fold in the flour. Place small spoonfuls, leaving space in between as the cakes will expand, on the baking tray. Bake for about 5 minutes until lightly browned.

Let sit on the baking sheet for about 5 minutes before carefully lifting onto a wire rack to cool completely.

To make the glacé icing, whisk the warm water into the icing sugar, along with a few drops of vanilla until you have a smooth runny icing. It should be thick enough to coat the back of a spoon, but still runny.

Spread half of the cooled cakes on the bottom sides with raspberry jam, just enough as not run out the sides when sandwiched. Sandwich them together with the 'un-jammed' cakes to make a ball shape.

Have ready the dessicated coconut in a shallow bowl. Dip the filled cake balls into the icing, turning carefully to coat and gently lifting out with a fork. Drop them into the bowl of dessicated coconut. Gently turn to coat completely with the coconut.

Carefully place onto a wire rack to set.

Spiced Fruit Loaf

This simple but delicious sweet bread is something I make sure I always have in my bread bin. Its great for those times when an unexpected guest turns up and you need something to give them with their cup of tea. Simply cut some slices of this loaf, lightly toast and smother in butter and you have sweet treat that will delight.

Ingredients:

8 oz (250g) self raising flour
4 oz (110g) dark brown sugar
8 oz (227g) mixed dried fruit (raisins, sultanas, currants etc.)
1 Egg (beaten)
2 tsp ground mixed spice
2 tbsp marmalade
1 cup of strong, hot tea, cooled
milk to mix as necessary

Dried fruit needs to be soaked ('steeped') in the tea overnight, or for at least 2 hours, before you begin this recipe!

Method:

Set oven to 180C / 350F / gas mark 4

Line 9" x 5" loaf tin with greaseproof paper

Mix all dry ingredients together in large mixing bowl.

Add egg, marmalade and fruit mixture/tea and stir together well with wooden spoon. Add enough milk to allow mixture to pour slowly into loaf pan.

Bake in the oven for 30 - 40 minutes until golden brown.

Allow to cool before removing from loaf tin. Slice and serve with butter.

Edinburgh Foggy Pudding

This has to be one of the easiest desserts I know. Simple and comforting, this is enjoyed by the whole family young and old.

Ingredients:

300 ml (1/2 pint) double cream
15 g (1/2 oz.) caster sugar
Few drops vanilla essence
50 g (2 oz.) ratafia biscuits (coarsely crushed)
25 g (1 oz.) flaked almonds (roughly chopped)
15 g (1/2 oz.) flaked almonds (for decoration)

Method:

Place the cream, sugar and vanilla essence in a bowl and beat until stiff.

Fold in the crushed biscuits and nuts, then divide between four serving dishes.

Decorate with the flaked almonds for decoration, chill and serve.

Scotch Whisky Mince Pies

Christmas would not be Christmas without the mince pie. These sweet little offerings are loved by just about everybody I know and I every year I make three or four batches to keep us going over the festive season. By the way, the mincemeat can be made months in advance of Christmas and when you do make it your home will smell amazing for weeks.

Ingredients:

Mincemeat Filling:

225g (8oz) apples, peeled, cored and chopped
4oz shredded suet
14oz dried mixed fruit
4oz candied peel, finely chopped
6oz dark brown sugar
Zest and juice of one orange
Zest and juice of one lemon
1oz finely chopped almonds
2 teaspoons mixed spice
½ teaspoons cinnamon
¼ teaspoon nutmeg
3 tablespoons Scotch Whisky

Method:

To make the Mincemeat:

Combine all the ingredients, with the exception of the whisky in an oven proof bowl.

Cover with a muslin cloth and leave to infused for 12 hours, or overnight in a cool place.

Pre-heat the oven to 120ºC.

Remove the muslin cloth and loosely cover the bowl with tin foil and put in the oven.

Leave the mixture to heat through for 3 hours to let the flavors develop, then take out of the oven to cool, stirring occasionally to help blend the ingredients together.

Once cool, add the whisky and store in an airtight container in a cool dry place.

Best eaten within a year of being made.

To make the pies:

Preheat the oven to 180°C.

Flour an even surface and roll some shop bought shortcrust pastry as thin as you can.

Cut the pastry into 8-10 3 inch rounds and the remaining pastry into strips for the lattice topping, ensuring you re-roll the trimmings.

Line the cake tins lightly with butter and dust with flour, then gently fit a 3 inch pastry round into each tin.
Fill these with the mincemeat mixture until level with the top of the tin.

Dampen the edges of the lattice strips with water and press lightly onto each pie to form the top of the pie.

Brush the lattice lids with milk.

Bake for 25-30 minutes until light golden brown.

Cool on a rack and dust the tops with icing sugar. Store in an airtight container.

Delicious served hot or cold with a dollop of freshly whipped cream.

Glazed Yum Yums

Yum Yums are Scotland's version of the doughnut. Instead of being made into a ring they are twisted into a spiral, a bit like Gemelli pasta (but much bigger) and with a sugar glaze. They can be found in any high street bakery and are extremely inexpensive but my homemade ones are the best.

Ingredients:

500g strong white bread flour
2 sachets (or 14g) fast action yeast
8g salt (one heaped teaspoon)
30g sugar
250mls water
1 medium egg
100g unsalted butter, chilled and diced

Oil, for frying
More flour, for rolling

Icing:

250g icing sugar, sifted
60ml (4 tablespoons) water

Makes 14-16 Yum Yums

Method:

In a large bowl, weigh out the flour, salt and yeast. Lightly rub the salt and yeast into the flour on opposite sides of the bowl, then rub in the sugar.

Dice the chilled butter into thin pieces. Add this to the flour and lightly stir the butter into the flour.

Add the water and the egg to your mixture and mix using a wooden spoon until begins to come together. Then, use your hands to mix until your dough has mopped up all the flour. Cover your bowl with cling film (or a wet cloth) and rest for at least half an hour at room temperature.

When the dough has rested flour a work surface and roll your yum yum dough out into a long rectangle. Turn your rectangle so the long side is facing you. Take both ends, and fold them into the middle. Then, close the whole thing like a book. Roll out again and repeat the whole folding process until your lumps of butter have disappeared (3-5 times). Wrap your dough in cling film and put in the fridge for another half an hour to rest.

Once rested, roll your dough out one final time on a floured surface into a big rectangle. Cut into strips of about six inches. To each strip, make a cut down its length, but leaving at least a centimeter attached at both ends. Twist this round into a spiral Yum Yum shape.

Leave to rest on an oiled surface in a warm place for at least an hour, until doubled in size. Near the end of the rest, make the icing by mixing the icing sugar and water, then prepare the oil

Shallow or Deep Fry your Yum Yums until a golden brown on each side. As soon as they're done, remove from the oil and brush liberally with the icing. Leave to cool completely on a cooling rack before enjoying.

Daredevil Deep Fried Mars Bars

This definitely is not a traditional Scottish dessert, however I thought I'd add this to my recipe book because this 'dish' has been getting quite a reputation in Scotland over the last few years. Many people believe it to be a myth that some fish and chip shops serve up a deep fried Mars Bars with a side order of chips, poking fun at the unhealthy diet the Scots are portrayed to have. But, alas, it is true, I have seen it with my own eyes, some chippies are doing it. Take your own life in your hands and try this recipe for Deep Fried Mars Bars. I urge you not to have it with a portion of chips.

Ingredients:

2 Mars bar
115g plain flour
10 tbs water
1 pinch salt
1 cup vegetable oil

Method:

Mix together the flour, water and salt into a smooth batter mixture with no lumps.

Place a small saucepan on the stove and pour in enough oil to just cover the Mars Bar.

Heat at a low temperature. Drop in a little pinch of batter, if the batter rises, bubbles and browns it is ready.

Using tongs dip the Mars Bar into the batter mix, covering the entire bar.

Place it in the saucepan and shallow fry for 1 minute or until crunchy and golden.

Remove and place on a plate with paper towel so excess oil can be soaked up.

Serve straight away bur WARNING!!! the middle will be very runny and VERY HOT.

Cranachan

Apart from haggis I don't think there is any dish more Scottish than Cranachan. This luscious desert full of cream, raspberries, whisky, oatmeal and honey is a blend of Scotland's finest natural ingredients that should be an advert for the country. Make this once and it will you dinner party finale for years to come.

Ingredients:

1lb/500g raspberries
6 tbsp whisky
3oz/75g pinhead oatmeal
3 tbsp Heather Honey
1pt/600 ml Double cream

Method:

Spread oatmeal on a baking sheet and toast in a medium oven until crisp for 3-6 minutes.

Leave to cool.

Whip the cream until it is thick but not stiff.

Blend all the raspberries (except 2 which are for decoration) until they form a smooth purée.

Combine oatmeal, whisky, honey, cream and raspberries.

Spoon the mixture into tall glasses

Chill for an hour or two before serving.

Just before serving, decorated if you wish with freshly whipped cream, a few fresh raspberries and drizzled with a wee bit honey.

Shortbread

No Scottish cookbook should be without a recipe for shortbread. The little butter, sweet biscuits are served up with tea and coffee throughout the land as a little treat. Be warned!!! One is never enough!

Ingredients:

1lb (500g) plain flour
1lb (500g) self raising flour
1lb (500g) butter
8oz (225g) caster sugar
Half teaspoon salt

Method:

Cream the butter and sugar together.

Combine with the sieved flour and salt. Use finger tips and do this gently.

Shape into 2 rounds with your hands.

Put on a baking tray.

Pinch the edges with your finger and thumb to give a nice finish.

Prick the base all over with a fork.

Bake in a low oven, 140c/ 275f / Gas 1 for around 1 hour.

Leave to cool, cut into the required shape.

Turn onto a wire rack.

Scottish Butter Tablet

For everyone with a sweet toot there is nothing better than a wee bite of Scottish Tablet. This sweety is sometimes compared to the better known dairy fudge, but Scottish tablet is more crumbly, sugary affair. Make this recipe and enjoy the naughtier side of life.

Ingredients:

2lbs (1 kg) Granulated Sugar
4 oz (113g) Unsalted Butter
One 14oz (396g) can of Condensed Milk
8 fl. oz (227ml) of Milk
1 fl. oz (3 dssp) Natural Vanilla Essence

Method:

Lightly grease a baking tray (11 x 19 inches works well) with butter and set aside.

Put the sugar and milk into a fairly large, heavy stainless steel saucepan (mixture will double in quantity as it heats).

Stir together. Add the butter and condensed milk and stir again.

Put the pan on a medium-high heat and bring mixture to the boil, stirring occasionally.

Once mixture comes to the boil, reduce the heat until mixture is boiling gently.

Continue to let it boil for around 20 - 30 minutes, still stirring occasionally.

Remove saucepan from the heat and add Vanilla Essence

Beat the mixture vigorously for 4 - 5 minutes, or until the mixture starts to feel more 'stiff' and 'gritty' under the spoon.

At this point the Tablet is ready to be poured into the baking tray you prepared at the beginning.

Allow mixture to cool a little and then mark it off into bars, or squares with a sharp knife.

Tablet is ready to eat when fully cooled.

Sláinte

Thank you so much again for reading my book and I sincerely hope you have enjoyed trying out these recipes. If you live in Scotland I hope these recipes have rekindled you love of Scottish food and If you are from further afield I hope to welcome you to Scotland one day and spoil you with our generosity.

~ Sláinte

Margaret Mochrie

Don't forget to check out my other book in the series " <u>The Wee Scottish Recipe Book</u>"

12745863R00022

Printed in Great Britain
by Amazon.co.uk, Ltd.,
Marston Gate.